The Ultimate Guide t

Lacey La

Copyright Lacey Lane 2015

Lacey Lane has asserted her right under the Copyright, Designs and Patents Act 1988 to be identified as the author of this work.

This book remains the copyrighted property of the author, and may not be redistributed to others for commercial or non-commercial purposes.

Table of Contents

Introduction
How to Reduce Your Energy Bills
How to Save Water
Frugal Food
Saving Money at Christmas
How to Get Free and Cheap Stuff
Exercise for Free
Cheap Dates and Days Out
Holidays
Saving Money on Car Care
Frugal Weddings
Frugal Babies
Recycling
Random Frugalness
Connect with Lacey Lane
Acknowledgements

The Ultimate Guide to Frugal Living

Hi! I am here to share a range of money saving tips ranging from reducing fuel bills to recycling. I hope you enjoy this book and I hope it helps you to live a more frugal life.

How to Reduce Your Energy Bills

Don't waste energy and money when boiling a kettle. Boil the amount of water you need. This is a simple but effective way of saving money.

When making a cup of tea you may need more water than is required for the tea to cover the element in the kettle. Don't waste this hot water, make use of it. For example, the excess can be used in a hot water bottle to warm up the bed or snuggle up on the sofa. Or put the unneeded hot water in a flask for later use.

In the winter before you turn up the heating make sure you are wearing warm clothing. What's the point in having the boiler turned up high and wearing shorts and a T-shirt? Have the boiler on a lower heat setting and wear a jumper.

Only switch on your heating when it's needed. Heating isn't needed when you are in bed or not at home. Most modern boilers have a timer installed. Use your timer so you don't waste energy and money. Make sure your frost stat is turned on in cold weather. Your heating will switch on to prevent your pipes freezing up if it gets too cold.

If you don't have central heating - get it installed. Central heating is more economical than using gas fires and immersion heaters. The cost of having the central heating installed will be recouped with the money you will save on your heating bills.

Radiator insulation panels will significantly reduce heat loss through external walls by directing the heat from the radiators back into the room.

After you've been cooking leave the oven door open to warm up your kitchen.

After bathing, leave the hot water in the bath tub. The hot water will give extra heat in your bathroom.

Electrical appliances left on standby use power; turn them off at the wall/unplug them when they are not in use.

For security reasons I leave some lights on a timer. I recommend this for safety but to save power and money turn off unneeded lights.

If there are lights that you regularly use for security and safety purposes, consider fitting energy–saving bulbs.

A well-insulated house will save you money and lower your carbon footprint. Loft, cavity wall, and floor insulation prevent heat escaping from your house.

Insulate your hot water pipes and water tank to keep the water warmer for longer.

Use draught excluders to prevent warm air escaping from the house through the gaps under your doors. You can get draught excluders to use on your letter box and key hole.

As soon as it goes dark outside draw your curtains. This will prevent heat escaping through windows.

Where possible, line-dry your laundry.

When possible, use a clothes horse to dry laundry, rather than a tumble dryer, which is heavy on energy use.

If it's a warm day lower the spin setting on your washing machine.

Use the washing machine on the coolest setting possible.

Freezers work more efficiently when full. If there is space in your freezer fill up some plastic food storage pots with water and use these to fill the freezer. You can also place empty cardboard food containers, like pizza boxes or ice-cream containers back into the freezer. As long as the space is occupied the container doesn't have to actually have anything inside.

Use a slow cooker instead of a gas or electric cooker. Slow cookers are cheaper to run.

Use a carpet sweeper instead of a vacuum cleaner. The only power a carpet sweeper will use is elbow grease.

How to Save Water

Find out from your water company if you can have a water meter fitted - external to the home. It may sound extravagant, but it is normally free. An external water meter registers the use by the individual household and it is only then the water you use that you pay for - and there are no 'average use' charges to consider.

Share bath water or take a shower together. You will use less water. This will reduce your energy too because less water is heated.

Use bath water to water plants or flush the toilet.

After bathing wash your dog in the used bath water.

It may be possible to divert your waste water from your bath into an outside water butt. This will save lots of water, which can be used for watering plants or cleaning the patio.

If your shower is over your bath put the plug in the plug hole. You can then use the water for flushing your toilet.
When you are waiting for the water to warm up in the shower, put a bucket under the running water. Save this water for watering plants, cleaning or flushing the toilet.

Take a shower where possible, which will save money, energy and time.

When taking a shower wet your body and hair and then turn of the shower while you wash yourself. Then turn on the water to rinse.

If you don't have a shower put some water in a bowl and stand or sit in an empty bath. Use a flannel and the water from the bowl to give you an all over body wash.

Don't flush every time you go to the toilet. Consider the method used by Dustin Hoffman and Barbra Streisand in the comedy movie, 'Meet the Fockers'. What is the method? 'If it's yellow, let it mellow. If it's brown, flush it down.' This is especially useful for when using the toilet during the night.

Put a plastic bottle filled with water inside your toilet cistern. This will reduce the amount of water used every time you flush.

Make sure your toilet cistern isn't leaking. This is easy to do. Put some food dye inside the cistern and leave it for a while. If the dye appears in the toilet bowl without flushing, you have a leak.

Use a water butt to collect rain water for watering your garden instead of using a hose pipe.

When you run the hot tap cold water will come out first. Collect this for rinsing veg, watering plants or for making cups of tea.

If you are cooking and need to drain water, for example, draining pasta, use the water for watering plants or flushing the toilet.

If you get through a lot of washing up it will be more economical to use a dishwasher. Put dirty plates etc. in the dish washer and wait until you have a full load before washing.

Make sure you have a full load of laundry before washing so you don't use extra water doing two half loads.

To prevent washing unnecessarily wear your clothes more than once. Use your nose and eyes. If it doesn't smell, and it looks clean where it again.

After showering don't throw your towel straight in the laundry basket. Dry yourself off and leave the towel to air dry and it will be fine to use another couple of times at least.

When brushing your teeth or shaving, don't leave the tap running.

Fix leaky taps.

To see if you have any leaks turn off all water appliances. Take a meter reading. Wait for 4 hours and take another reading. If the reading has changed there is a leak.

Urine can be used as a natural fertilizer for plants. This benefits the plants and saves water.

Get in touch with your water company. A lot of water companies give away freebies to save water in the home.

Start the dishwasher just before going to bed. The national grid is less busy and the electricity is cheaper through the silent hours. The items will be cool enough to lift straight out first thing in the morning.

Frugal Food

Do not shop while hungry. You are far more likely to buy food you don't need.

Plan your meals and make a shopping list. You will be less likely to buy things you don't need.

Don't assume well know branded food is better than supermarkets' cheaper own brand equivalent. Next time you go shopping, swap the expensive well-known brands for the cheaper ones and you will find you will be pleasantly surprised.

Buy in bulk. Supermarkets often try to deceive us with "buy one get one free" or similar offers. Sometimes though this can be beneficial. Stock up if the item is something that you will use and has a good "Best Before" date.

Remember not to accept that milk, yogurt, bread and other fresh foods presented at the front of a display is the best. If the store staff are doing their job properly and rotating stock, the longest dates will be at the back and the shortest dates will be pulled to the front to try to sell them off first.

Don't waste money buying bottled water, drink tap water.

Go foraging. This is super fun and provides free food. You can forage for berries, nettles, apples, pears, rosehip and many more. You can make delicious jams and teas etc.

Switch to packed lunches for school meals and lunch breaks at work.

Don't worry if food is past its Best Before date. Most food is good to use for a long time, especially frozen food and tinned food.

Eggs last a lot longer than their Best Before date. Here's a quick test to find out if your eggs are fresh enough to eat: Fill a bowl with cold water. Gently place the egg in the bowl. If the egg floats to the top don't eat it.

If you want gravy to go with your vegetables use the hot water that your vegetables were cooked in instead of boiling the kettle.

If your jar of jam has started to go mouldy, scoop off the layer with the mould.

If your cheese has started to go mouldy, cut off the mouldy part.

Have a "use up" week. This is great for using up random bits of food and clearing your cupboards, fridge and freezer. Don't be afraid to make meals from random bits and bobs. It may not be conventional but it will still be tasty and it will avoid waste too. Random left over vegetables can be used to jazz up meals. Left over mushrooms can be added to a pizza. Left over peas can be used to make mushy peas to go with chips. By doing this it will prevent unnecessary buying and waste.

Best Before dates are a guide so should be interpreted as such. If bread for example, is up to two or even three days beyond its Best Before date, do a visual check of it and provided it looks okay, it can still be used for toasting. Use more caution with Use By dates. Food labelled with Use By dates are the type of foods that can easily produce food-poisoning bacteria.

Over ripe bananas make a good, natural face mask. Mash up the banana and rub it over your face. Leave on for 10 minutes and then rinse off with warm water and pat dry.

Lots of food can be frozen. Make yourself familiar with what can be frozen so that you can cut eliminate waste. Knowing what is good to freeze comes in handy when shopping. A lot of supermarkets offer big reductions on food that is nearing the end of its best before/use by date. Most of these can be frozen to use at a later date. Freeze leftovers from meals at home to prevent waste. Freezing food in reusable plastic containers where possible to reduce waste from packaging. Always freeze food/drink in usable portions. Below is a list of some of the not so obvious foods that can be frozen.

Butter and margarine can be frozen for up to six months. Freeze in original packaging or put a freezer bag/plastic container. Decant small amounts into ice cube trays and put in a freezer bag for when only small portions are needed. Defrost in the refrigerator.

Cheese and frozen for up to six months. Some cheeses may crumble after freezing but they will taste good and be safe to eat. Cut cheese into useable chunks (so it's not wasted after defrosting) and freeze in plastic containers or freezer bags. Defrost in the refrigerator. Cheese can be grated before freezing. Frozen grated cheese can be put straight on bread and put under the grill for cheese on toast.

Bread can be frozen for up to six months. Defrost at room temperature. Bread can be toasted from frozen.

Milk can be frozen for up to three months. When freezing milk leave room in the bottle for expansion. Defrost milk in the refrigerator and give it a good shake before using.

Fresh herbs can be frozen for up to twelve months. Chop the herbs as desired and spread the herbs out on a baking tray. This stops the herbs from freezing in big clumps. Once frozen transfer into a plastic pot or freezer bag. Herbs can also be frozen in an ice cube tray with a little left over stock or a little water. This is perfect for casseroles, soups and stews.

Berries including blueberries, blackberries, strawberries, raspberries, cranberries, elderberries, gooseberries, currents (red, black and white) can be frozen for up to twelve months. To freeze place a thin layer on a baking tray to prevent clumping and freeze for two hours then place in a freezer bag or plastic container. Defrost in the refrigerator overnight or use from frozen for baking. Hull strawberries before freezing. Once defrosted berries may be softer than fresh fruit but they are still edible and tasty.

Grapes can be frozen and defrosted the same way as berries. Alternatively freeze them in an ice cube tray with water and add the grape ice cubes to your favourite drink.

Bananas can be frozen for up to two months unpeeled and up to four months peeled. The skin of an unpeeled banana will go black when frozen but the inside will still be fine to eat. It will go mushy once defrosted, but this is great for making smoothies or adding to ice cream or yogurt. Defrost covered up at room temperature for roughly one hour. Alternatively peel the bananas before freezing and freeze in plastic container or freezer bags. These will be less mushy when defrosted. Freeze them one layer at a time so that they don't stick together.

Homemade pancakes and waffles can be frozen for up to three months. Freeze individually for 30 minutes to prevent them from sticking together. They can then be put together in a plastic tub. Heat in the microwave from frozen until piping hot.

Soups, broth and stock, can be frozen for up to six months. Freeze them in plastic containers. Defrost in the refrigerator overnight.

Fresh peppers and chilli peppers can be frozen for up to a year. They can be frozen whole. You can remove seeds and chop them before freezing if you wish. They can be used from frozen when cooking.

Chilli can be frozen for up to six months. Store in plastic containers and defrost overnight in the refrigerator.

Rice and pasta can be frozen for up to three months. Store in plastic containers. Defrost overnight in the refrigerator.

Pesto can be frozen for up to three months. Freeze in an ice cube tray and once frozen transfer to a plastic container. Defrost at room temperature for twenty minutes.

Mashed potato can be stored in plastic tubs in the freezer for up to six months. Defrost overnight in the refrigerator.

Eggs can be stored in the freezer for up to three months. Crack the eggs and beat together. Freeze in an ice cube tray. Once frozen transfer to a plastic tub. Defrost overnight in the refrigerator.

Homemade casseroles and pasta meals such as lasagne and macaroni and cheese can be frozen for up to three months. Freeze portions in plastic containers and defrost overnight in the refrigerator.

Yogurt can be frozen in its sealed original container for up to three months. Yogurt can be decanted into smaller plastic containers before freezer. Ice cube trays are perfect for freezing small portions. Once frozen transfer to a plastic container. Defrost overnight in the refrigerator and stir before eating. The texture may be different but the taste will be the same. Frozen yogurt is great for making smoothies and for use in cooking.

Juice can be frozen for up to three months. Freeze in plastic containers or bottles leaving room for expansions. Defrost overnight in the refrigerator and stir before drinking.

Avocadoes can be frozen for up to three months. Puree the avocadoes with a little lemon or lime juice and it's perfect for a dip. Freeze using an ice cube tray and then transfer to a plastic tub. Defrost in the refrigerator overnight.

Hummus can be frozen for up to three months. For small portions freeze using ice cube trays and then transfer to a plastic container. Defrost overnight in the refrigerator. Stir before eating.

Garlic cloves can be frozen peeled or unpeel for up to three months. Store in plastic containers. Garlic can be used from frozen for cooking.

Saving Money at Christmas

Buy tags, wrapping paper, Christmas cards and decorations in the post-Christmas sales.

To be extra frugal make tags out of old Christmas cards and use pages out of old magazines instead of wrapping paper.

Send e-cards instead to save money on cards and postage.

Buy presents in the post-Christmas sales and other clearance sales throughout the year.

You need not buy presents for everyone (aunts, uncles, cousins, and cousins' children). Only buy for immediate family. Make an agreement in advance to not buy for each other.

Agree on an amount to spend on presents and stick to it.

Homemade gifts are great. They are personal, fun to do and can save you money.

Keep receipts for all gifts bought. In the event of a faulty or unwanted gift it can be returned instead of sitting on a shelf gathering dust.

If you receive an unwanted gift this can be put up and given to someone else next Christmas. Make sure you keep a note of who gave it to you so you don't give it back to them by mistake.

When buying stocking fillers for children buy things they will need in the near future. Toiletries, books for school, stationary, shoes, clothes etc. are things that you may have to buy your children anyway. By buying these for Christmas you will kill two birds with one stone.

Consider doing a "secret Santa" instead of buying gifts for everyone in your group of friends. Put everyone's name in a hat. Each person draws a name at random and buys a present for that person. It's lots of fun because it's a big secret and everyone will receive a present and only have to buy one present. Set a limit. A "pound shop secret Santa" is great for a giggle and a great price too.

Lots of Christmas foods have long shelf lives on them. Buy these in the post-Christmas sales.

Christmas is a time where typically a lot of meat is bought. Get together with family and friends to create a "meat group" and approach your local butcher. You may be able to get a discount for bulk purchases.

If you are having a big Christmas get together share out the cost. Organise between you who will provide the starter, main, desert and drinks.

Put money in a savings account every week/month to use nearer Christmas for the things you can't buy until December.

Supermarkets and high street shops offer free loyalty cards. Use them to collect points throughout the year and use the points to buy presents/food. Remember; don't buy for the points because the points scheme may be withdrawn at any time. Buy your goods at the cheapest price and the points are a bonus.

How to Get Free and Cheap Stuff

For freebies check out websites such as: https://www.freecycle.org and https://ilovefreegle.org/
These websites were created to reduce waste and stop things being sent to landfills. There are plenty of gems to be found on these sites: furniture, clothing, books, toys, kitchen equipment etc.
The websites are easy to use. Either respond to someone else's advert or create one of your own either offering something or asking for something.
www.facebook.com is a good source for freebies. Search for your local freebie page and you'll find it will work in a similar fashion to freegle and freecycle.

There are numerous buying and selling websites and Facebook groups. Although the items won't be for free you can still pick up a bargain. Search online to find websites/groups in your area.

Check out your local charity shops, car boot sales and jumble sales. One person's rubbish is another person's treasure. Have a good rummage and you might pick up a bargain.

Exercise for Free

Make the most of where you live and go for long walks. Make use of local parks, forests or beaches.

Walk instead of driving. Not only will you be exercising for free but you won't be spending money on petrol.

A lot of local gyms offer free day passes to encourage new members. Make the most of the free passes. You don't have to sign up to become a member afterwards.

Cycle to work instead of driving.

Search for exercise equipment on local freebie websites.

Use a skipping rope. This is something that can be done in your own garden for free and the price of the skipping rope would be minimal.

Always take the stairs instead of using an elevator.

Cheap Dates and Days Out

Go for a romantic walk with your partner (beach/park/woods/countryside/by the river). You could take a small picnic with you, so you don't have to pay for food while you are out.

Have a candle lit meal at home.

Have a romantic bonfire in the back garden. Get a fire pit or similar from a freebie website and collect waste wood (I see waste wood on freebie websites all the time). Buy a cheap bag of marshmallows and hey presto.

Have a candle lit bubble bath together followed by a sensual massage.

Have an indoor picnic.

Go online and search for free festivals/carnivals.

Go to the pub. This doesn't need to cost a lot. Go to your local so you can walk there and back. Once you are there make one drink last you a couple of hours.

For those of you who live by the sea, make the most of it. Go and spend a few hours on the beach. Relax together and when the weather is warm enough make the most of the sea too.

Strip card games at home are free and can add a bit of spice to your relationship.

Breakfast (or any other meal) in the garden.

Build a snowman/sand castles together (weather permitting).

Check online before you go on any days out. There are lots of free days out online and lot of places offer discounted rates for booking in advance.

Spend a night camping in your back garden with the kids. They will love the adventure.

Check out your local library. Libraries often host events such as book signings and book readings etc.

Go bike riding together.

Holidays

Go out of season if it doesn't affect children at school.

Go away for a week instead of two.

Book trains, ferries or flights well in advance and you can reduce the price by almost half in some cases.

Consider self-catering instead of package, but it depends on your requirements/expectations. If you eat and drink a lot an all inclusive package may suit you better. Do your research.

Visit friends or family who live in another part of the county. You will only need spending money and your travel fare.

Saving Money on Car Care

Don't be afraid to switch insurance providers. Shop around and you could save yourself a small fortune.

Buy de-icer after winter when it is at a reduced price and store it ready for the next winter.

Although windscreen wash is used all year round the price often reduced after winter. Stock up while it is on offer.

Empty your car. Excess weight uses more petrol so only keep necessities in the car.

Having the heating/air conditioning switched on uses more petrol, therefore it is important to dress accordingly.

Remove your roof rack when not in use. It's unneeded weight, and it disturbs the air flow which uses more petrol.

Accelerate and brake gently to avoid using excess petrol.

Drive in the correct gear.

Make sure your tyres are at the correct pressure.

Wheel alignment is important. This can be done by a mechanic relatively cheap and can save you a lot of money in the long run.

Proper maintenance can help your car run more efficiently. It's possible for you to do some maintenance yourself. Make sure you have a maintenance hand book for the jobs you can do and take your car to a trusted mechanic for the things you can't.

Check the oil regularly and change/top up when needed, making sure you use the correct oil.

Maintaining your coolant system is important. The level of coolant needed is indicated on the reservoir under your car's bonnet.

Lift sharing is a good idea. Speak to your colleagues. There maybe someone who lives near you and works at the same time as you. Take it in turns driving to work. You will both use half the amount of petrol and there will be less wear and tear on your cars.

If you have children walk them to school where possible. This will give them exercise and save you petrol. If it's not possible to walk organise a car pool with other parents whose children live close by and go to the same school.

Before joining a motoring organisation, check your credit card terms and conditions. Some credit card issuers include roadside rescue, but locating it in the small print might take a while.

Frugal Weddings

Visit high street stores. A lot sell bridal ranges which cost a fraction of the price of having a dress made or buying a designer dress.

Search through your local freebie websites and charity shops. You may find a dress or suit for free or cheap.

Don't have specially made invites. Buy suitable card and envelopes from your local stationery store and print your own, which will be less expensive and more personal. Or buy a pack of invites from your local card shop or send e-invites.

For photography and hair and makeup approach local college/university students. Because they are starting out in their careers and wanting to build up their portfolios you will be able to get cheaper rates.

Most photographers charge an arm and a leg for prints and albums. Instead of buying these expensive prints and albums ask for the photos to be put on a cd and print them out yourself for a lot less. Search online for special offers with online photo printing companies.

Instead of having wedding cars, ask a family member or friend to drive you to your wedding.

Instead of having gifts from family and friends, request their talents instead. E.g., if your auntie is a cake maker, ask her to make your cake. If your sister is a dress maker, ask her to make your dress. If your uncle is a DJ, ask him to be the DJ at your wedding reception.

Don't hire people to decorate your venue. Get a group of family and friends together and do it yourself.

Use your local supermarket for your flowers. This will be cheaper than wedding flowers from a florist.

Consider getting married on a week day. A lot of venues offer cheaper packages to encourage more business on their quieter days. Winter weddings can also be cheaper.

If you get married late in the day, you can avoid having a sit down meal and the costs it incurs. A party with a buffet will be cheaper. Alternatively skip the party and only have a wedding service.

Another possibility to save money on food is to have the wedding service and then a pub lunch with immediate family only.

If you decide on a buffet for your meal you can make a list of food for the buffet and ask the guests to each bring something from the list instead of a gift.

Fish and chips can make a great alternative to the usual wedding meals. Contact your local fish and chip shop in advance and arrange delivery.

You need not have your wedding reception to be at a fancy hotel. There are plenty of nice church halls and social clubs that will cost a lot less. You could hire out a room in a pub or have the reception at home.

If you get married in a church, try to time it so you get married after someone else's wedding. You can then take advantage of the flowers being in church from the previous wedding.

Haggling is important. Bartering is possible for most aspects of the wedding. If you can't get the price knocked down try to get extras thrown in for free. For example if the bride and bridesmaids are all having beauty treatments for the big day ask for a group discount. If it's a last minute wedding haggle on the venue price. The venue owners would more than likely give a discount or thrown in some freebies than have no sale so close to the date.

Remember your wedding is your special day and should be how you want it. Don't invite people just to make them happy and don't feel pressured by family to have things at your wedding that you don't want. This will avoid unnecessary costs.

Frugal Babies

Breast feed where possible. It's free.

Charity shops, jumble sales and car boot sales are great for bargain clothes. Babies grow out of clothes quickly so there's no point wasting money on expensive clothing.

Local freebie sites are a great source for baby equipment (pushchairs, baby seats, cots, clothing, toys etc.).

Talk to family and friends. They may have unwanted baby clothes/equipment from when they had their babies.

Prepare a baby gift list. It is more than likely that your family and friends will want to buy a present to welcome your new baby into the world. With a prepared gift list you are more likely to receive what you need and you can avoid unwanted gifts.

If you are planning on having more than one baby keep everything to hand down to your younger children.

Reusable cloth nappies are cheaper and better for the environment that disposable nappies.

Instead of buying jars of baby food make your own. When cooking a meal make more than you need. Blend the excess and freeze. Freeze using an ice cube tray to make small portions and transfer into a plastic container once frozen.

Don't spend a fortune on your babies at Christmas and birthdays. Buy them a small inexpensive gift or something they need. Put the rest of the money you would've spent on an expensive gift into a savings account for your child. They will then have money when they need it in the future.

To save money on child care do a child care swap with friends. On your day off take care of a friend's child and vice versa.

Where possible work when your partner isn't at work. Take care of the children when your partner is working and your partner can look after the children while you are working.

Offer services in exchange for child care. In exchange for family or friends looking after your children you can do something for them. You could walk their dog, cut their grass, clean their car etc.

Recycling

Recycle as much as you can. Recycling is better for the environment and can save you money. Here's some ideas you can use around the home.

Save old jam/coffee jars. These can be used for storage at home or in the garage. They are handy for storing screws, buttons, nails etc.

When you have finished with your tubs of ice cream keep the empty tub. They can be used to store food in your freezer.

Empty toilet rolls and kitchen rolls can be shredded up to put in your compost bin.

Save your vegetable peelings, tea bags, egg shells and coffee grinds for your compost bin.

Empty tissue boxes are great to stuff your used carrier bags into to keep them neat. Pull them out as you need them just like you would a tissue.

If you know anyone who eats in a fast food restaurant get them to keep the children's meal box. This can then be used to make you own children's meal at home.

The mesh bags that your vegetable come in can be used as scourers for when you are washing up.

Old socks are great to use as dusters.

Empty perfume bottles can be left in wardrobes or draws to fill the air with a lovely scent.

Make use of the envelopes from your bills and junk mail. Cut them up into small squares and use as note paper for shopping lists etc.

Use old clothing to make new things; bags, peg bags, cushion covers, patchwork quilts etc.

Use your local recycling centre for any recyclable waste that you can't make use of.

Random Frugalness

Before buying beauty products or cleaning products, use up what is already available at home.

Don't waste small left over bits of soap. Keep your left over soap bits; grate them up and melt them in a saucepan (use a low heat). Mix together and pour into a mould. You don't need to buy special moulds. You can use the bottom of an old plastic milk bottle. Leave the mixture to cool and go hard in its mould and then you will have a new bar of soap.

Supermarket shelves are full of very expensive cleaning products for around the house. A quick search of the internet will provide you with many easy to make recipes which will cost you less than shop bought alternatives.

Looking good doesn't need to cost a fortune. Look online for recipes for DIY facemasks, bubble baths, shower gels etc.

When visiting a salon ask if any trainees need practise. You could barter and pay less for a trainee doing your hair cut, waxing etc.

Don't buy expensive cleaning products to clean your silver jewellery. Rub toothpaste over the silver, leave for a while and then wipe off with a clean damp cloth.

When you can't get any more tooth paste out of your tube, cut the bottom off and you'll be able to squeeze more out. The same can be said for moisturisers, foundations and most things that comes in this type of tube.

Create your own "swap shop" event. Organise your friends and family to get together. Everyone should bring along something they don't want and it can then be swapped with someone else's unwanted item. Remember; one person's junk is another person's treasure.

It is important to shop around before buying anything. Prices can vary from vendor to vendor so it is important to have a little patience and not buy from the first shop/website you come across.

Know when to haggle. If you are buying from a local selling site never pay the asking price. It is possible to haggle in some shops too. Haggling is a must when renewing any kind of contract (mobile phone, broadband, insurance etc.).

Use spare cash to clear your debts starting with the biggest debt first. By doing this you will reduce the amount of interest you have to pay. Once your debts are paid off concentrate on your mortgage. Over pay every month and you will reduce the term of your mortgage and the amount of interest you pay. (Check the terms and conditions of your mortgage first. Some mortgage providers limit the amount you can over pay.)

Learn to say "no." If your children are constantly saying "can I have this?" you may find it hard to say "no." Be strong and say "no." Encourage them to save up their pocket money to buy things they want. Encourage them to shop around to get it cheaper elsewhere. This way as well as saving yourself money you are teaching your children the value of money too. This is a valuable lesson they need to learn.

Before buying anything ask yourself if you need it. Also ask yourself if there is a cheaper alternative? Can you get the same quality for less money elsewhere?

Do you pay for TV channels you don't watch? Assess what you watch and if you don't watch all that you are paying for switch to a cheaper package.

Do you use a mobile phone? Assess how many minutes you use a month and how many texts you send. Compare this to how many minutes/texts you pay for in your contract. Next do your research and compare deals. If you are a light user you may find it cheaper to switch from a contract to pay as you go. If you do still need a contract make sure you are not paying for more than you will use.

Grow your own fruit and veg. This is great for keeping active and saving money. Don't worry over the size of your garden. It doesn't matter if you only have a patio or balcony. There are still plenty of options you can explore. You could even go into shares with a neighbour. Make a plan between you of who will grow what produce and then share the crops between you.

If you have a garden, consider getting hold of a hand-mower, even if you have an electric model. A hand-mower doesn't use electricity, whereas an electric model uses a lot. A hand-mower creates an instant free exercise opportunity.

Quit smoking and drinking alcohol. As well as being bad for your health these are an expensive habit.

Connect with Lacey Lane

Thank you for reading The Ultimate Guide to Frugal Living. I hope you enjoyed it. These valuable tips will help you live a more frugal life, save you money and help the environment.

Would you like to take part in my next frugal book? All you have to do is visit my Facebook page and send me a message with your frugal tips. The senders of the best tips will be acknowledged the tips featured in the next book.

To connect with Lacey Lane please visit:

www.facebook.com/laceylaneauthor

www.twitter.com/LaceyLaneAuthor

Other books by Lacey Lane:

The Revenge of the Pumpkins

The Little Book of Horrors

Acknowledgements

Thank you to my partner for always being there for me. You are my rock and you mean more to me than you'll ever know.

I would also like to thank my beta readers:

L.J. Redding of Pelican Proofing
Lucinda E Clarke
Tom Benson   http://www.tombensonauthor.com

Thank you to A.V. Scott for her help with the cover design.

Printed in Great Britain
by Amazon